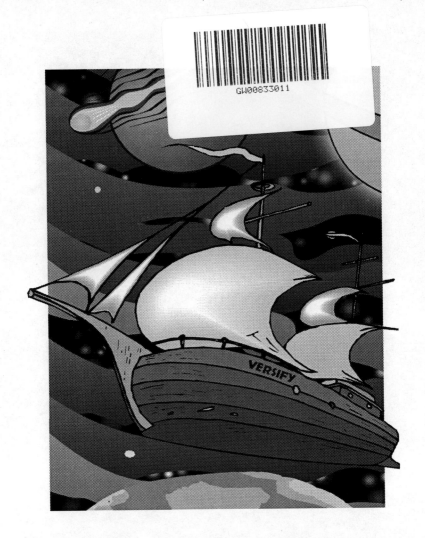

VERSIFY

POETIC VOYAGES
NORTH DEVON

Edited by Dave Thomas

First published in Great Britain in 2001 by
YOUNG WRITERS
Remus House,
Coltsfoot Drive,
Peterborough, PE2 9JX
Telephone (01733) 890066

HB ISBN 0 75433 312 4
SB ISBN 0 75433 313 2

FOREWORD

Young Writers was established in 1991 with the aim to promote creative writing in children, to make reading and writing poetry fun.

This year once again, proved to be a tremendous success with over 88,000 entries received nationwide.

The Poetic Voyages competition has shown us the high standard of work and effort that children are capable of today. It is a reflection of the teaching skills in schools, the enthusiasm and creativity they have injected into their pupils shines clearly within this anthology.

The task of selecting poems was therefore a difficult one but nevertheless, an enjoyable experience. We hope you are as pleased with the final selection in *Poetic Voyages North Devon* as we are.

CONTENTS

Sophie Ann Field	32
Shaun Taylor	33
Sophie Jefferies	34
Jacob Johnson	35
Adam Hughes	36
Thomas Green	37
Chloe Iliffe	38
Darren White	39
Alexander John Dovell	40
Jack Benson	41
Heather Belinda Cowell	42
Andrew James Roberts	43
Joshua Hulston	44
Bob Aldridge	45
Robyn Kusmidrowicz	46
James Naston	47
Hannah M Lovering	48
Gemma Catherine Jefferies	49
Michelle Saunders	50
Robert Allcoat	51
David Coggin	52
Abigail Rice	53
Amanda Gubb	54
Sam Draper	55
Hayley Brown	56
Maria Johns	57
Ashllyn Musgrove	58
Melissa Spencer	59
Daniel Batchelor	60
Thomas Hack	61
Sam Hughes	62
Lewis Darch	63
Jamie Boast	64
Kieran Sanders	65

Forches Cross Primary School

Chantalle Galliford	66
Kathleen Morgan	67

Newport Community Primary School

Stephanie Phillips	104
Dale Thomas	105
Sadie Yeo	106
Naomi Hanson	107
Christy Woollacott	108
Lucy Lazarus	109
Kate Moscardini	110
Jessica White	111
Zoe Thayre	112
Kayleigh Andrews	113
Peter Hill	114
Joe Hunter	115
Shauni Draper	116
Jamie Easterbrook	117
Bradley Barbrook	118

Pilton Bluecoat Junior School

Luke Austen	119
Jamie Prouse	120
Hayley Johnson	121
Faye Young	122
Kealeigh Roddis	123
Elaine Loveridge	124
Sophie Winfield	125
Kathryn Marie Venn Munns	126
Sam Furse	127
Pippa Friend	128
Jadine Watson	129
Hannah Cluley	130
Jody Fewings	131
James Cann	132
Rebecca Cooke	133
Roxanne Kerner	134
Mikayla Brookes	135
Louise Mason	136
Kirsty Burge	137
Hannah Bowden	138
Leanne Dean	139

Katherine Marshall	140
Kelly Watts	141
Imogen Curtis	142
Gina Corti	143
Stacey Vaughan	144
Susannah R E Bay	145

Sticklepath Primary School

Mark Wonnacott	146
Jessica Billson	147
Rebecca Louise Derbyshire	148
Gavin Andrew	149
Veronica Holland	150
Zoe Simmonds	151
Lucy Sleeman	152
Simon Hanson	153
Natalie Elston	154
Robert Lewis	155
Sam McCreadie	156
Lydia Brown	157

Two Moors Primary School

Natalie Dundh	158
Tom Hawkins	159
Class E2	160
Sophie Andrews	162
Thomas Drysdale	163
Sammy Head	164
Lyndsay Rachel Ryan	165
Thomas Hutter	166
Vicky Preston	167
Ben Daniel	168
Jordan Thomas	169
Zoe Bates	170
Alice Bennett	171
Trevor Davis	172
Andrew Jones	173

The Poems

THE VISIBLE BEAST

You can't miss him.
He's as big as the Eiffel Tower,
And as wide as Hadrian's Wall.
Teeth as sharp as ten razors,
Still can't miss him at all.
Eyes like red lasers,
Breaths like ten gas tanks,
And burning down his caves.

He's green and slimy,
And can't hide anywhere.
He cannot run,
You see him wherever you go.
He crushes towns,
And stamps around.
He squashes cars in all the towns,
And crushes them like the scrap heap challenge.

He might be beside you,
Or might not.
Don't go near him,
Or he will go near you.
He's trying to climb up bedroom walls,
Or knocking at your door.

He's trying to see you,
Though you can't see him.
He may be behind you,
And may be in front.
He will scare you right behind you,
And lurking right behind you.

So be scared,
'Cause you're going to die.

Philip Chapple (9)
Bickleigh-on-Exe CE School

THE VISIBLE BEAST

Its feet are like little knives
Its skin is green, orange and slimy
Its bones are pointing up like sharp knives
Every time it gasped fire came out its mouth
Its eyes are like stones that glare at you
Its head is like a stone bashing down a path before it
It runs as fast as a cheetah
Its ears are like sharp knives
Its green and slimy skin could tear your bones to bits.

Rachel Reed (10)
Bickleigh-on-Exe CE School

THE VAMPIRE

The vampire wakes from his graveyard
He goes out every night
To look for people to see what he could find
He was looking at the window to see what he could find
And all that he could find was some bones
His teeth were like ice
His hand was as white as snow
No one could see him, he was invisible
He had no friends, then there was somebody coming
The person saw him
His heart was stomping like a drum
But I don't know why he was scared because he was gone.

Alex-Jade Budd (8)
Bickleigh-on-Exe CE School

THE BEAST

It lives in a cave, pitch-black and only lets itself out after sundown.
It has teeth as sharp as razors and as big as a child.
Its body is as big as Hadrian's Wall and as wide as two football pitches
stuck together.
Its tail has a huge python on it.
Its breath is as large as 1,000 flame throwers.
So watch out, he might be there with 190 eyes watching you.
But look out! That was a close shave.
Now he returns to his pitch-black cave.
It stalks itself and minimises as big as a leech.
When the python on its tail bites you die immediately.
But then as soon as you think you're safe,
It strikes with a lonely cry.
It will nibble you to death
And when he has finished you he'll let out an electrifying roar.

Christopher Pring (9)
Bickleigh-on-Exe CE School

The Beast!

Its head is as big as six tables,
He has six feet that were the size of wheelbarrows,
Four legs the size of the biggest tree stumps,
Six feet tall and seven feet wide,
Its head has four eyes bigger than footballs,
If you let it catch you it would eat you like a crumb.
You would not want to see it,
Because you'd never see again.

Peter Randerson (9)
Bickleigh-on-Exe CE School

THE WATER WHISPERING

If you dare to swim in the Loch Ness
You will see the beast
He has a hollow stomach so beware
The lake goes frozen like a thousand knives stabbing you
His frozen breath gently rubs your body
If you feel that, it won't be a fish
You will run and hide but he will snatch
But who is he?
He is just a harmless beast
He is not what you think it might be.

Joshua Binks (9)
Bickleigh-on-Exe CE School

BEFORE THE WOLF EATS YOU

It runs through the forest with blood dripping from its hungry teeth.
It howls in the night while eyeing up its next meal.
He tears his meat up with his massive claws and teeth.
It starts to rub his blood from its teeth because it took a long time
to catch his meat.
If you were something he caught, you would be dead in a second.

So watch out for the wolf!

Jordan Hewitt (8)
Bickleigh-on-Exe CE School

INDIAN EARTHQUAKE

Hunger in villages
People crying
Disorder struck
Death!

Kelsey Watts (10)
Bishops Tawton CP School

UNTITLED

Ground splits open
Buildings topple
Families killed.

Ryan Felkin (10)
Bishops Tawton CP School

INDIAN EARTHQUAKE HAIKU

Huge cracks, holes open
People falling, getting trapped
Rescue services.

Jade Poole (10)
Bishops Tawton CP School

INDIAN EARTHQUAKE HAIKU

Cries under rubble,
Families separated,
Tragedy, sadness.

Tara Birch (11)
Bishops Tawton CP School

INDIAN EARTHQUAKE HAIKU

Earthquake shaken place,
Screaming, crying, hurt people
Families split up!

Chantelle Hadland (11)
Bishops Tawton CP School

STORM

Stacked up high, the clouds
throw knives of sharp lightning
Splintering sparks of yellow light
flicker ferociously!

Thunder shouts out his mission
Boom! Boom! Like a general
and his army of lightning
Crash! Clang! The guns of war
spout from the clouds, clash!

Over the hills the war began
when all the dark cumuli-nimbus
clouds gathered in search of land!
'Land ho!' shouted Thunder the general.
So war was close!

Raging clouds rumbled over town
as more clouds were gathering
The people ran frantically to their houses
screeching and wailing!

Mumbling thunder rolls along the town sky
Clashing lightning demolishes the stars
as clouds cover them in black.

Cherry Bromfield (10)
Bishops Tawton CP School

WINTER DEVASTATION

Peaceful, silent place,
Glistening trees,
Crunchy snow,
Magical landscape,
Happy, joyful people,
Hot filling food,
Outside,
Skiing,
Train up the mountain,
Loud noise,
Crash, flames, smoky gas,
Terror rushing like flames,
Struggles of desperation,
Screams,
Cries,
Happiness disappearing,
Choking,
Falling,
Motionless bodies,
Shocked,
Mournful village,
Crying friends,
Candles in memory,
Devastated hearts,
Silent, quiet, sad.

Georgina Treanor (10)
Bishops Tawton CP School

Mountain Disaster

Beautiful landscape,
Filled with soft snow,
Glitzy ice caps sparkling in the sun,
So peaceful, soothing, gentle.
Cascades of snow,
Filling the landscape around them,
A gorgeous atmosphere,
Cold and calming,
Dress in warm clothes of fur and wool,
Clamber on the train,
Filled with excitement, joy,
Until!
Suddenly a halt,
Flames spread.
Devastation,
Terror.
Black smoke chokes,
No escape.
Joy and happiness torn away,
Thoughts of death
Going through their mind.
Sobbing, crying,
Tragic devastating disaster.
Heartbroken, miserable, tearful people,
Ambulance sirens.

Lauren Howard (11)
Bishops Tawton CP School

INDIAN EARTHQUAKE

The earth was shaking
Buried under the rubble
Lots of people died.

Nicky Hayward (10)
Bishops Tawton CP School

THE LAST RIDE

A beautiful day,
Glaciers smoothed in snow.
Wonderful stone cold ice,
Gleaming on the points of glaciers.
Glistening trees.
Dripping cream - like snow,
Soothing down sides of mountains.

Suddenly!
The train halts.
Fire turns to scorching flames,
Bodies turn to black dusty ash.
Smoke puffing out of mouths,
Breathing in smoke.
Horrified screams,
1000 degrees burning bodies!
The train melted to liquid.

Sobbing friends,
Weeping relatives,
Distraught families.
A terrible disaster,
It was some people's *last ride!*

Jas Kalsi (10)
Bishops Tawton CP School

AUSTRIA'S DISASTER

Smooth, cold, deep, glacier, snow.

Tragedy, tragic, screaming, crying, freezing,
Explosions, people melting, sparkling, mountains, ashes.

Sad, amazed, puzzled, tragic.
I open my curtains,
Everything is covered in a thick blanket of icing.
Everybody went on a train ride.
When we were just about to reach the top,
The train blew up,
Everybody was choking to death.

Craig Ridd (11)
Bishops Tawton CP School

DISASTER IN AUSTRIA

I woke up,
Everything in snow,
Glittering, sparkling ice,
Spectacular!
People skiing.

People on a train,
Halfway up when
Bang!
The train - blown-up,
Smoke out of the tunnel,
Everywhere.

Crying, sad people,
As no one survived.

Sophie Bailey (10)
Bishops Tawton CP School

Austrian Disaster

A perfect day.
Layers of thick white snow
Covering all.
Drops of dew,
Glistening on damp, spiders' webs.
No one could think of anything possible
To sadden this perfect day.
With joyful skiers leaving on a train
For a fun day out.

All was fine,
But halfway up,
It ground to a halt.
Bang!
Immense heat.
Black smoke.
Limp people dropping.
Terrified screams
As scorching flames
Burned them alive.

In a shocked village
Of disbelief.
Weeping friends
And distraught family.
With a candle in the street
For every priceless life lost.

Pip Scott (10)
Bishops Tawton CP School

INDIAN EARTHQUAKE

The ground is breaking
Buildings crumbling, people scream
But no one can hear.

Sam Brace (10)
Bishops Tawton CP School

THE AUSTRIAN DISASTER

Peaceful, silent place.
Glittering snow, soft and gentle like swan's down,
Glaciers sparkle in sun rays,
Mountain peaks, sprinkled with icing sugar,
Sun floating in a sky of blue.

Horror, terror struck!
People fall motionless to the ground.
Fireproof material melting,
Destruction, devastation!
CO_2, swirling, suffocating,
Choking, coughing, death.

Ambulances, stretchers, oxygen masks,
Weeping takes over, relatives dead.
Bewilderment . . .
Why?
How?
When?
Candles spread,
Flickering for dead.
Will it happen again?

Laylah Morris (11)
Bishops Tawton CP School

SISTER

I have a big sister
Boys wouldn't want to kiss her
She's cool but tall
She wants to be a vet
But she wants to have a pet.

My sister cares and shares
She is very talkative and very walkative
She's cool by the pool
I don't know what I would do
With another big brother of a sister.

Danielle Clancey (10)
Combe Martin Primary School

MY SISTER

I have a big sister
I never would have kissed her
She doesn't share
But she doesn't care
I wish she had a blister.

My sister is eleven
I wish she was seven
She's not that tall
She's never been cool
She'll definitely not get to Heaven.

Her boyfriend's called Mark
They play in the dark
They laugh a lot
But then forgot
They were meeting some friends at the park.

Zoe Chadwick (10)
Combe Martin Primary School

LITTLE SISTER

I have a little sister,
Boys never would have kissed her.
She is so strange, I want a little brother for a change.
She's not very caring and she hates sharing.
Sometimes I wish my little sister was never there.

Danielle Doran (10)
Combe Martin Primary School

ANIMALS

Animals here
Animals there
Animals everywhere
Animals that fly very high
Like birds in the sky
Animals that live low
Like elephants trampling the place
Animals that live underground
Like armadillos digging their holes
Animals here
Animals there
Animals everywhere.

Callum Bardsley (7)
Combe Martin Primary School

NIGHT-TIME

When I'm in bed
I think I hear
The moon whistling
Twinkly stars in the sky
I hear crashing
Things downstairs
What could it be?
What could it be?

Natasha Caswell (8)
Combe Martin Primary School

HIDING

Cats under the table
hiding from the dogs
Mice under the floorboards
hiding from the cats
Birds under the nest
hiding from the cats.

Amber Simons (8)
Combe Martin Primary School

WHALE

If you ever, ever, ever
see a whale
you must never, never, never
touch its tail
For if you ever, ever, ever
touch its tail
you will be sent to jail.

Joe Read (8)
Combe Martin Primary School

WHEN I SAW A TIGER

When I saw a tiger
it gave me quite a fright
When I tried to stroke him
he gave me a bite
When I saw a tiger
he gave me quite a scare
When I saw a tiger
it jumped up and grabbed my hair.

Kieran Chugg (8)
Combe Martin Primary School

FIRE

Fire is bright
  Fire is light
    Fire is scary
      Fire is darey
      Fire is crackly
    Fire is rattly
  Fire it hot
Fire is what?

Ben Lawson (7)
Combe Martin Primary School

BABIES

Babies are sweet,
Babies are kind,
Babies cry time to time,
Babies don't eat proper food,
But sometimes they cry and cry,
They like black and white,
They also like pretty colours.

Sophie Ann Field (9)
Combe Martin Primary School

STRAWBERRIES

Going to pick strawberries
Growing in the fields
Sheep are feeding
Eating grass
Men come to bring them in
The sheep running
Down the hill.

Shaun Taylor (9)
Combe Martin Primary School

THE BEACH

I am going where the stream
Slowly goes into the sea
The sea crashes against the rocks
Where the seagulls are stealing food
And the seaweed is slippery.

Sophie Jefferies (8)
Combe Martin Primary School

SNAKE

Slithery tongue,
Slimy skin,
Razor-sharp fangs,
Thirteen foot,
My snake is great.

Jacob Johnson (7)
Combe Martin Primary School

COMBE MARTIN

Hollands Park -
Playing football
With my mates
Combe Martin -
Peaceful village
On the beach
Waves crashing
Against the rocks.

Adam Hughes (9)
Combe Martin Primary School

FANTASTIC FLYER

A fantastic flyer
A stony starer
A weird waddler
A winged slapper
An excellent runner
A loud hisser
A scary attacker
A good biter
A catalogue
to make me a goose.

Thomas Green (9)
Combe Martin Primary School

THE DEEP BLUE SEA

The crashing waves
rush over the rocks
as the seaside boat docks
The crabs crawl
through the deep blue sea
White horses call to me
Up and down waves fall
I build a pond, the fish call
The mysterious things
in the deep blue sea
Where do they come from?
Where do they go?

Chloe Iliffe (8)
Combe Martin Primary School

DOGS

Dogs run fast
Dogs are the best
Dogs walk 'round
But don't wear vests.

Dogs never talk
Dogs always play
Dogs forever bark
Dogs never eat hay.

Darren White (8)
Combe Martin Primary School

MY CAT

Cuddly, cute
Sits in a boat.

Scared of a dog
Runs from a hog.
Sits on a log.
Sings to a frog.

In at midnight
Out at day.
He'll give you a fright.
He's black as night.

His name is Bodger
That's my cat.

Alexander John Dovell (7)
Combe Martin Primary School

BIKING ALONG THE TARKA TRAIL

Biking along the Tarka Trail,
All lumpy and bumpy.
Sloshing through puddles,
Very muddy.
Wearing a helmet,
Pedalling hard.
Got home,
Splattered with mud!

Jack Benson (8)
Combe Martin Primary School

DREAMS

Close your eyes into another world.
A place just for your imagination.
Have bad, good, even sad dreams.
Have kind, even dreamy dreams and baby dreams.
Dreams of far away,
Dreams of my bedroom,
Dreams of the sky,
To wake in the morning.

Heather Belinda Cowell (8)
Combe Martin Primary School

MY LOVE

My love is strong for you,
My love is the best,
My darling don't leave me,
My sweetums come to me,
My dear love,
The best thing to happen to me
Come here.

Love from your Valentine.

Andrew James Roberts (8)
Combe Martin Primary School

IN THE DARK

Scary, spooky dark
Dogs howling,
Wind blowing,
Rocks smashing against the wall.
Frightened!
I hate the dark.

Joshua Hulston *(7)*
Combe Martin Primary School

CROCODILE, CROCODILE!

He trims skin
He swims
He chills you
He kills you
He thrills you
He traps you
He's sneaky
Snap!

Bob Aldridge (7)
Combe Martin Primary School

GRANDAD

Crinkly faced,
he sits on his favourite chair
in the jagged pub,
silently drinking Stella.

He sits comfortably
asleep on his creaking, rocking chair,
like the cat curled up on his lap.
He jumps up like a firework
exploding and walks desperately
to his favourite pub for a lovely drink.

Robyn Kusmidrowicz (10)
Combe Martin Primary School

GRANDAD

As Grandad sits comfortably in the study
polishing his guns, in his wide relaxing armchair,
dosing as if he was a cat lying by the radiator.

Gradually lifts himself, a slow snail, as he moves
slowly outside to sit with the dogs
as they lie under the rose bush catching the shade
before the sun takes over their spot.

Hairless, apart from a grey moustache
catching all the pasta from the minestrone soup.
Smells of Old Spice aftershave.
Bends down shaking, to pick up the ball
to roll for the dogs.

James Naston (11)
Combe Martin Primary School

NANNY

Made-up face, as she sits on the
antique rocking chair
with cushions all around her,
like a glamorous Barbie.

She works all day,
then picks me up,
takes me home
and stuffs me with dinner and sweets.

She sits comfy, she watches
EastEnders and Coronation Street,
like a statue,
with a glass of brandy in one hand.

Hannah M Lovering (10)
Combe Martin Primary School

GRANDAD

Bald-headed, he sits in his decrepit old chair,
a silhouette of yellow dust,
silently reading, reading last year's newspaper,
he sits satisfied as though in a world of his own.

Eyes sparkling like spring mountain water
gleaming in the crystal-clear air
he turns to you like a flower leaning towards the sun.

Gemma Catherine Jefferies (11)
Combe Martin Primary School

GRANNY

Wrinkly fingers, wrinkly toes,
as she's looking at them,
rocking in her rocking chair,
drinking red wine,
as her cat curls up on her lap.

She starts painting her pale nails,
in dark blue nail varnish,
as she eats a bag of ready salted crisps,
with a cookie.

She has curly hair,
with her very pale face
staring at the TV,
watching EastEnders.

Michelle Saunders (10)
Combe Martin Primary School

GRANNY

Bald-headed,
with a curly grey wig on,
rocking back and forth in her antique
rocking chair, a pendulum in a clock.
Watching Coronation Street on her 50 year old TV.
Holding her whisky in a late Victorian glass,
as if she doesn't know what it is,
as if she has a memory span of a goldfish.

Robert Allcoat (11)
Combe Martin Primary School

GRANDAD

Fat-faced, solidly sitting looking out into the world.
Deathly listening to the cobwebby radio.
Making a cup of tea with a crooked hand.
He goes to the pub and has a laugh with his mates.
Cautiously he drinks his Budweiser.
He slomps into his armchair watching The Bill, brainlessly.
Fading into the chocolate-covered Milky Way.

David Coggin (9)
Combe Martin Primary School

GRANDAD

Loving smile,
he harmlessly milks the spotted cows.
A sweet darting humming bird.
He works proudly.
An angel flying through the sky.

Grey-haired,
he sits at the table,
like a careless sleeping lion.
He eats his delicious porridge
like a stuffed animal.

Abigail Rice (9)
Combe Martin Primary School

GRANDAD

His round, crooked back curves like a camel's hump
He sits poking his big belly at the TV scoffing chocolate and beer
As he watches TV his belly grows like someone blowing up a balloon
His brown teeth get browner as he eats chocolates
His big, round glass is like a football shining in the TV light
His house as hot as fire begins to get colder as night falls.

Amanda Gubb (10)
Combe Martin Primary School

GRANDAD

My limping grandad
who counts his sparkling money
like a man in a bank
Watches the timeless snooker
in front of the dull TV
Limps to his snooker room
sets up the snooker balls
Plays snooker
limps back to the kitchen
and has a cake and a cup of tea.

Sam Draper (10)
Combe Martin Primary School

GRANDAD

Crinkly faced
and grey haired
as he fiercely walks to the pub
desperate to have a drink
a hungry monkey going through the bins.

Blue eyed
he carefully walks back
while his gentle daughter
opens the squeaky door
She takes his ripped coat off
and sits quietly watching football
cheering like an angry, rough bull
seeing a sheet of red.

Hayley Brown (9)
Combe Martin Primary School

WORKING HARD

Wiry haired
he fixes my toys
like a busy elf
like a sheepdog in the fields
wise as an owl he works like a beaver
sawing wood
like a crocodile
crunching his food.

Maria Johns (9)
Combe Martin Primary School

SEEING GRANNY

Granny she kisses with wrinkled lips
Puffy mouth like fish lips, all wet
She grabs your face and squeezes me.

Ashllyn Musgrove (11)
Combe Martin Primary School

SEEING NANNY

Skinny-handed,
she sits rounded up as if she was a ball
just sitting in a chair
solidly watching Coronation Street.
Then she sips her flaming hot coffee
as if it was fire.
Then sewing away she goes like a spider making its web.
White-socked and ginger, a cat called Socks walking
crouches down like a furious tiger about to pounce on its prey
and sits on nanny's lap - a cat curled up.
Nanny takes one stroke deeply in the cat's fluffy, hairy fur,
the cat purrs like a machine gun.
Nanny is tired,
she does one deep yawn
like cat was whining.
Finally nanny goes to bed.

Melissa Spencer (9)
Combe Martin Primary School

GRANDAD

He's got white hair in the shape of ear muffs
He is bald on top
He's got a plump belly
He is very kind and always gives me pocket money
When he goes down the road to get his newspaper
he buys me some sweets
He likes tea and watches a lot of the news
Sometimes he does watercolour paintings
and he makes model boats
He takes his boat to a pond and sails it.

Daniel Batchelor (11)
Combe Martin Primary School

CATS

Cats - I'm touching cats
- small cats
- big cats
- fat cats
- thin cats
- black cats
- white cats
- dirty cats
- smelly cats

What sort of cats do *you* like?

Thomas Hack (8)
Combe Martin Primary School

ANIMALS, ANIMALS, EVERYWHERE

A slippery snake
A toothy tiger
A big brown bear
A jumping jaguar
A leaping lion
A gorgeous giraffe
A famous frog.

Sam Hughes (7)
Combe Martin Primary School

THE SPACEMAN

He shoots
through the clouds
and he races
through the stars
and he lands back
on Mars.

Lewis Darch (8)
Combe Martin Primary School

CATS

Cats keep cool
Cats are careful
Cats keep clean
Cats hear their way back
Cats climb trees
Cats have nine lives.

Jamie Boast (7)
Combe Martin Primary School

THE LITTLE SNAKE

There was once a little snake
who had to bake a cake
he had toothache
but he made a mistake on the cake
so he went back to being a little snake.

Kieran Sanders (7)
Combe Martin Primary School

LOVE AND SUCCESS

Love is red with beautiful silver hearts in it
Love smells of strawberry liquid with splashes of perfume
Love tastes of a chocolate cake with a sprinkle of icing
Love sounds like a lovely violin playing sweet, soft music
Love feels like a fantasy world with the sun shining on your eyes
Love lives in your heart safe and fine.

Joy is yellow like the sun, so happy
Joy smells like a piece of fresh bread
Joy tastes like a crunchy caramel sweet
Joy sounds like a child singing cheerfully
Joy feels smooth like someone's hair
Joy lives in the bright sun.

Chantalle Galliford (10)
Forches Cross Primary School

EMOTIONS

Love is scarlet red,
It smells of hot chocolate.
Love tastes like a bowl of soup,
It sounds like a blackbird singing,
It feels warm like a warm bed.
Love lives in the heart of a human.

Playfulness is bright green,
It smells of strawberries.
Playfulness tastes of candy and sweets,
It sounds of a robin singing.
It feels like a smooth cushion.
Playfulness lives in a warm sunny garden.

Joy is spearmint,
It smells like a daffodil.
Joy tastes sweet,
It sounds like a sparrow singing.
It feels like a warm cushion.
Joy lives in a heart of a bird.

Happiness is mango orange,
It smells like a daisy.
Happiness tastes like candy,
It sounds like a blue tit singing.
Happiness feels smooth and soft,
Happiness lives in everyone.

Kathleen Morgan (10)
Forches Cross Primary School

MY EMOTIONS

War is bloody red
It smells like mouldy bread
It tastes like burnt toast
War sounds like a fight in the park
It feels rough and sharp
It lives in the planet called Mars.

Love is bright red
It smells like sweet strawberries
It tastes like strawberry ice cream
It feels smooth and gentle
It lives in your heart.

Ricky Creek (10)
Forches Cross Primary School

EMOTIONAL THOUGHTS

Love is peach
It smells of tulips
It tastes of chocolate
Love sounds like a bluebird
It feels soft and squishy
Love lives in our hearts.

Hope is silver
It smells like perfume
It tastes of toffee
It sounds like an ocean in a seashell
It feels soft and smooth
Hope lives in the heart of the sun.

Happiness is yellow
It smells of grapes
It tastes of apple
Sounds like birds singing
It makes me feel smiley
It lives in our homes.

Kayleigh Leeming (10)
Forches Cross Primary School

EMOTIONS

Love is calming
It smells like fresh roses
Love tastes like a sweet strawberry
It sounds like birds singing sweetly
Love feels like all your dreams have come true
It lives in your heart

Peace is violet
It smells like tulips
Peace tastes like candyfloss
Peace sounds like relaxing music
It feels soft and smooth
Peace lives in a sunny meadow

Joy is bright yellow
It smells like fresh flowers
Joy tastes like hot chocolate
Joy sounds like a robin singing
It feels like a relaxing bubble bath
Joy lives in the heart of a dolphin

Hate is dark black
It smells like black burnt toast
Hate tastes bitter and sour
Hate sounds like bombs going off
It feels like a hedgehog's spines
Hate lives in a volcano.

Kelly Hamilton (10)
Forches Cross Primary School

EMOTIONS AND FEELINGS

Disease is black and moulding green,
It smells like rotten fish and eggs.
Disease tastes sour and bitter,
It sounds like a chalk screeching across a blackboard.
Disease feels like gunge and it is all bumpy,
It lives in a dark cave.

War is bright red,
It smells like the inside of a cannon just been fired.
War tastes like burnt up gases,
It sounds like blasting cannons.
War feels like burning hot gunge,
It lives in black cannons.

Loneliness is dark green,
It smells like rotten potatoes.
Loneliness tastes like clay,
It sounds quiet.
Loneliness feels hard
And it lives in a dark corner.

Jacob Kriehn (11)
Forches Cross Primary School

MY EMOTIONS

Death is blood red,
It smells like a burnt down house.
Death tastes bloody and brutal,
It sounds like children crying for their lives.
It feels like a heart in the palm of your hands.
Death lives in the soul of an evil man.

Hate is dark black,
It smells like a chamber full of poisonous gases.
It tastes bloody and bitter,
It sounds like a million guns firing off at once.
It feels like sheep's brains.
Hate lives in the deep depths of an evil man.

Alastair Hart (10)
Forches Cross Primary School

EMOTIONS

Peace is light blue,
It smells like bluebells,
Peace tastes sweet,
It sounds like whales singing,
Peace feels relaxing,
Peace lives in a garden filled with flowers.

Happiness is orange,
It smells like fresh flowers,
Happiness tastes like candy,
It sounds like a robin singing,
Happiness feels smooth,
Happiness lives in your heart.

Love is red,
It smells like red roses,
Love tastes like a sweet raspberry,
It sounds like a blue tit singing,
Love feels soft,
Love lives in a sunny meadow.

Joy is pink,
It smells like daisies,
Joy tastes like fresh strawberries,
It sounds like a sparrow singing,
Joy feels gentle,
Joy lives in everyone.

Rebekah Leach (10)
Forches Cross Primary School

EMOTIONS

Love is red,
It smells like a red rose,
Love tastes sweet,
It sounds like a heart beating,
It feels weird and smooth,
Love lives inside a golden treasure chest.

Hope is yellow,
It smells like a buttercup,
Hope tastes like vanilla ice cream,
It sounds like a singing bird,
It feels soft and smooth,
Hope lives in a sunny meadow.

Ross Parkhouse (11)
Forches Cross Primary School

EMOTIONS

It is yellow
It smells like a sunflower
It tastes like a lemon sweet
It sounds like a bluebird singing
It feels like a bear's coat
It lives with us everywhere

Death is dark
It smells like a dead frog
Death tastes like worms
It sounds like an earthquake
It feels like a snake
Death lives in a black hole
And we all have it.

Vanessa Williams (10)
Forches Cross Primary School

MY FEELINGS

Hope is red
It smells like a big, red, red rose
It tastes like a lovely big red strawberry waiting to be picked
It sounds like someone has just won a lot of money
It feels like me getting everything I want
Hope lives in a big garden covered in flowers.

Joy is orange
It smells like all the things that I want in this world
It tastes like every kind of sweets
It sounds like happy children playing in the park
It feels like someone who is never sad
Joy lives in the heart of a human.

Sharon Sim (10)
Forches Cross Primary School

MY EMOTIONS

Fear is sky blue,
It smells like freezing ice.
Fear tastes cold like frost,
It sounds like a heart beating.
Fear feels like ice melting in your fingers,
Fear lives in your heart.

Death is coal black,
It smells hot like a fire.
Death tastes like sweat,
It sounds like a bang of a gun.
Death feels like slimy slugs,
Death lives in the sewers.

Hope is light yellow,
It smells like a sunny day.
Hope tastes like cherries,
It sounds like laughter.
Hope feels like water dripping through your fingers,
It lives in God's heart.

Ben Huxtable (10)
Forches Cross Primary School

MY EMOTIONS

War is red
It smells like smoking cigarettes
War tastes like a gun that has just been fired
It sounds like someone shouting
It feels hard and warm
War lives under the ground

Hope is white
It smells like sweet cherries
Hope tastes like a sweet apple
It sounds like a sweet voice
It feels like a red rose
Hope lives in the heart of us.

Thomas Hearn (9)
Forches Cross Primary School

MY EMOTIONS

Death is black,
It smells like a rotting corpse,
Death tastes like slugs and flies,
It sounds like trombones played by amateurs,
Death feels wet and slimy,
Death lives in the sewers!

Hope is a sunny yellow,
It smells like freshly cut grass,
Hope tastes like fresh grapes,
It sounds like a harp,
Hope feels soft and bouncy,
Hope lives everywhere.

Passion is purple,
It smells like perfume,
Passion tastes sweet and juicy,
It sounds like a drumming rage,
Passion feels warm,
Passion lives in your heart.

Adrian Brayley (10)
Forches Cross Primary School

EMOTIONS

Hope is orange
It smells like a rose
Hope tastes like fish and chips
It sounds like a child singing
It feels soft
Hope lives in your heart.

Sadness is dark blue
Sadness smells like going-off strawberries
It tastes like a dead animal
It sounds like someone crying
Sadness feels like you when you are sad
Sadness lives in you and your friend.

Jimmy England (11)
Forches Cross Primary School

EMOTIONS

Love is a beautiful red,
It smells like a red rose,
It tastes like peaches, orange and bright,
It sounds like a blue tit, singing in the trees,
It feels like a swan's feather, soft and light,
It lives in a beautiful blue lake.

Joy is orange,
It smells like a white lily,
It tastes like honey, sticky and sweet,
It sounds like gentle waves,
It feels like a soft fur coat,
It lives in the clouds.

Hope is pink,
It smells like chocolate,
It tastes like bubble gum,
It sounds like birds chirping,
It feels like tissue, soft and silky,
It lives in a sunny meadow.

Happiness is yellow,
It smells like buttercups,
It tastes like strawberries,
It sounds like soft sand, blowing along the ground,
It feels like cat's fur,
It lives in the heart of the sun.

Vicky Emma Rafferty (11)
Forches Cross Primary School

AN EMOTION ABOUT WAR

War - it smells like a rusty old gun
War - it is the colour of black
War - it tastes like a stick of rock
War - it sounds like cars blowing up and thundering back down
War - it feels hard and sharp
War - it lives in the soul of a man and woman who are very angry
Don't fight!

Louis Rooke (10)
Forches Cross Primary School

THOUGHTS

Sadness is blue,
It smells like cold ice cubes.
Sadness tastes like ice cream,
It sounds like a baby crying.
It feels like the wind blowing, twisting and turning.
Sadness lives in a hole in the ground.

War is orange with red lava,
War smells like blood.
War tastes like wood,
War sounds like a shotgun bullet.
War feels like fire,
War lives in chimneys.

Thomas Woolacott (10)
Forches Cross Primary School

My Emotions

War is reddy-orange
It smells of gone-off blood
It tastes like dead bodies
It sounds like people crying for help
It feels like a cannon going off
It lives in the heart of the underworld.

Pain is red
It smells of dirty socks
It tastes of pain
It sounds like people laughing
It feels like you're dying
It lives in the North Pole.

Daniel Shapland (9)
Forches Cross Primary School

EMOTIONS

Fear is white
It smells like a dead sheep
It tastes like pig's sick
It sounds like booming rock songs
It feels like you've been stabbed in the heart
It lives in the heart of a ghost.

Death is red
It smells like a car on fire
It tastes like a bullet with blood on it
It sounds like fire engines
It feels like you've been shot in the head
It lives inside of a gun.

Karl Windsor (11)
Forches Cross Primary School

FEELINGS

Hope is orange
It smells sweet like flowers
It tastes like sweet honey
Hope sounds like bumblebees flying
It feels that you are dancing all the time
Hope lives in people's hearts.

Joy is yellow
It smells like a strawberry just been picked
It tastes like fruits of all kinds
Joy sounds like people laughing and joking
It feels like jelly inside you
Joy lives in people's lives.

Love is rose red
It smells like lots of sweets
It tastes of fruits in the sun
Love sounds like violins playing
It just feels like love
Love is in people's minds.

Natalie Parr (10)
Forches Cross Primary School

EMOTIONAL THOUGHTS

Death is red
He smells like hot fire burning away
It tastes like spicy fire in your mouth
It sounds like a giant roaring for help
It feels hot, hard and sharp
He lives in a volcano floating away.

It's grey like wool, it hopes to die
It smells like a dog rotten and gone
She tastes like hot fire floating in air
She sounds like a granny as well as a dragon
It lives in a dustbin.

Hope is yellow, sweet as can be
It smells like a flower with a daisy floating away
She tastes dry and sweet
It sounds like a heart singing in love
And she lives in a garden of peace.

Tanya McMinn (10)
Forches Cross Primary School

SKATEBOARDS

Skateboards whizz down hills,
Skateboards whizz down ramps,
Some go fast,
Some go slow,
Skateboards, skateboards, skateboards,
Go!

Jack Hutchens (8)
Newport Community Primary School

ROBOT

Once my dad brought us a robot,
A mad robot!
And this robot was in trouble.
First, when dad brought the robot,
They named him 'Naughty Tom'.
Now Naughty Tom was always up to no good.
First we told him to hoover up,
But he jumped up and down and broke the ceiling.
Oh, what next?
Then Mum said 'Go cut the grass,'
But he went behind Mum and cut her hair.
She looked like a robot,
And everyone laughed, 'Ha ha!
Take Tom to the dump.'

Lucy Hardy (8)
Newport Community Primary School

COLOURS OF THE YEAR

Black is the colour that I see in bed,
It's on the walls, it's on the floor,
It's even round my head.

The morning sky is bright and blue,
To and fro the clouds go by,
The yellow sun lights up the sky.

The morning dew looks wet and bright,
Shows up the flowers so red and white,
There's orange and purple and red and green,
So many colours all to be seen.

When autumn comes the colours fade,
Crispy reds and crunchy browns,
Golden yellow, tumbling down.

Frosty white and silvery sheen,
The colours of the year are there to be seen.

Alex Leonard (10)
Newport Community Primary School

OUR SWIMMING LESSON

'Come on, everyone, it's front crawl!'
Is what we hear the teacher bawl.
Breathe to the right, and tumble turn,
What stroke is next for us to learn?

Breast stroke, arms, push and glide,
Make sure your two hands touch the side,
Bubble, bubble, bubble, breathe,
The next few strokes we swim with ease.

Arms straight over, fingers high,
Head right back, look to the sky,
Alternate circles each arm makes,
Straight leg kicks is what it takes.

Dolphin body, arms right out,
'Legs together!' comes the shout.
Butterfly is the hardest one,
Speedwork next, and then it's fun.

Lesson's over, five minutes play,
That's swimming finished for today!
At least we know it's done us good.
Why don't you try it? Everyone should.

Rebecca Southam (9)
Newport Community Primary School

WATCH OUT!

Beneath the darkness
Of the sky,
Stands a body
With glowing eyes.
Keep houses locked
And always alight,
'Tis Hallowe'en
'Tis Hallowe'en.
She loves the darkness,
But hates the light,
Beware my friends
'Tis her night tonight!

Hannah Laycock (10)
Newport Community Primary School

THE LITTLE BIRD

There was a little bird, sitting in a tree;
Along came a cat and said to he,
'Little bird, little bird, come and join me.'
'Do you think I'm stupid? You will eat me!

Black cat, black cat, amber eyes staring at me,
Can you think of something else for your tea?
Like some crunchy biscuits, and a kipper from the sea,
For they will taste much nicer than me!'

Simon Pert (10)
Newport Community Primary School

BROTHER

Spine tingler,
Stress bringer.
Anger giver,
New top spoiler.

Heaven destroyer
Hell runner.
Food thrower,
Peace stunner . . .

But I love him!

Grace Rogers (11)
Newport Community Primary School

FOOTBALL

I really like football,
And running round the pitch,
If I ran too fast
I might just get a stitch.

I like to keep the ball
Under good control.
And if I'm playing really well,
I might just score . . .
A goal!

David Willoughby (9)
Newport Community Primary School

STRAWBERRIES

Strawberries big,
Strawberries small,
With a shawl of white and red,
They are juicy, so juicy,
I even take them to school.
Strawberries big,
Strawberries small,
Strawberries, strawberries, strawberries.

Chloe Parker (9)
Newport Community Primary School

TRAVELLING ROUND THE WORLD

I travel round the seaside,
I travel round the globe,
I travel round the United Kingdom,
I travel round the world.
I travel in a taxi,
I travel in a car,
I travel on a scooter,
I travel to Panama.
I travel on a ferry,
I travel on a cruise,
I travel on a plane
Which aliens call 'ooze'.
I travel to Africa, Asia, America too,
But I'd rather have a holiday in Kathmandu!

John Gayfer (9)
Newport Community Primary School

MONEY, MONEY, MONEY!

If I had a million quid
I'd buy a swimming pool with a lid
(To keep the neighbours out, you see).
Then I'd buy a panther, just for me.
I'd buy a butler, a maid and a cook,
And even someone to read me a book.
I'd also buy a cinema screen
To watch the films I haven't seen.
I'd buy new clothes every day,
No need to wash them, I'd throw them away!
A new car, or two, or three or four,
And if I fancy, maybe more;
A coach, a boat, even a train,
And to get back home
My own private plane.

You may just be wondering what you'd spend it on,
Sorry! Hard luck! I'm afraid it's all gone.

Ricky Hedge (10)
Newport Community Primary School

PARENTS

I hate parents,
They boss you around,
They even tell you off
When you don't make a sound.
They say 'Do this!'
They say 'Do that!'
They say, 'Go next-door,'
So I go next-door,
And they tell me off
For doing that!

Daniel Gerry (11)
Newport Community Primary School

CHOCOLATE LOVER

Cadbury consumer,
Mars bar muncher,
Twirl taster,
Crunchie cruncher,
Rolo rustler,
Lion Bar licker,
Caramel craver,
Pick 'n' mix picker,
Creme Egg counter,
Smartie smasher,
Galaxy gazer,
Button basher,
Fruit and Nut fanatic,
Snickers shopper,
Dairy Milk dreamer,
Chomp chopper.

Lucy Coleman (10)
Newport Community Primary School

HAMSTER

Fast runner,
Warm maker,
Run awayer,
Finger shaker.

Food cruncher,
Different colour,
Noise maker,
Food fluffer.

Peanut eater,
Day sleeper,
Nice sweetheart,
Night creeper.

Melissa Moore (10)
Newport Community Primary School

CHIPS

Baskets dipped in hot oil,
See my chips begin to boil,
Turning golden, crisp and light,
Oh what a wonderful delight!
Salt? Vinegar? Sauce? Yes please.
Now, watch me eat them as I tease.
Chips!

Rebecca Bater (10)
Newport Community Primary School

LET'S PRETEND

Let's pretend we're pop stars,
Let's pretend we're ghosts,
Let's pretend we're pirates
Sailing to the coast.

Let's pretend we're explorers,
Let's pretend we're on TV,
Let's pretend we're on a cruise,
Sailing out to sea.

Let's pretend we're fashion models,
Let's pretend we're in a submarine,
Let's pretend we're back in bed,
Floating in a dream.

Jennifer Kent (10)
Newport Community Primary School

BLACKBIRD

Blackbird, blackbird
Swooping high and low,
Come into my garden,
Please don't go.
How I love to watch you ,
As you catch a worm,
Even when the garden
Is snowy and firm.

Blackbird, blackbird
With your orange beak,
Where are your babies?
Playing hide and seek.
Hopping to and fro,
Up and down you go,
Blackbird, blackbird,
How I love you so.

Stephanie Phillips (10)
Newport Community Primary School

I Still Grow

The sun is hot
The snow is cold
The rain is wet
The wind is strong
The sky is blue
The grass is green
The seasons change
And I still grow.

Dale Thomas (10)
Newport Community Primary School

CLOUDS

Clouds are like pillows, fluffy and white,
Floating above us,
We gaze in delight.
Oh, how I wish we could touch them and see
Just how puffy and fluffy they really could be!

Sadie Yeo (11)
Newport Community Primary School

SEA OF FEELINGS

The sea is like a person,
He has feelings too.
His feelings rise to the surface,
They just come out of the blue.

Sometimes he's calm and gentle,
Sometimes as smooth as glass,
But when he's feeling angry
You'll sense the mighty blast!

When he's feeling moody
And his temper begins to rise,
The tide will begin turning
Before your very eyes.

A storm at sea is frightening,
You'll feel his mighty force.
It takes a brave captain
To steer the right course.

When his storm is over
He'll begin to settle down soon.
Maybe it's been all over nothing,
He'll be as calm and gentle as the lagoon.

Naomi Hanson (10)
Newport Community Primary School

CHOCOHOLIC

I'm a chocoholic,
My parents both agree.
Instead of eating one bar
I end up eating three!
I bought so much chocolate
I don't know which to pick,
I've eaten so much today
I'm feeling rather sick.
If someone wants to buy me some
And put me to the test,
Galaxy is my favourite,
It's better than the rest!

Christy Woollacott (10)
Newport Community Primary School

BUNNY MAD

It's funny what your pets can do
When you don't really have a clue.
For instance, when my bunny saw
How appealing was the door,
Ashamed to let it go to waste,
She thought she might just have a taste.

I didn't know she could make a leap
So high, and still land on her feet.
Right out of her cage and onto the chair,
But I don't think she really cared
As she jumped back down onto her brother,
And made him bolt, and dive for cover

And I'll never forget this,
When I was sad and needed a kiss
My bunny ran upstairs where I lay,
And did this, in a very nice way;
She jumped onto my bed quite joyfully
And jumped around all full of glee,
She licked my face, she licked my nose,
And later on she licked my toes!

Lucy Lazarus (10)
Newport Community Primary School

My Aunty Sonia's House

Sonia's house is such a mess,
It is enough to give you stress.
To give you more of a description
I shall start off in the kitchen.

Pots and pans, and washing up,
You cannot find a clean cup!
The kitchen bin is overflowing,
The pile of rubbish ever growing.

The lounge is like a Council tip,
You cannot find a place to sit.
So many toys are on the floor
It's a struggle to open the door.

You should see the pile of ironing
That would have my mum whining.
As rumour has it, one day soon,
They might just tidy one small room!

Outside, the tale does not improve,
In the garden you can't move.
But hayfever sufferers won't shed a tear,
The grass hasn't yet been cut this year!

To end this story set in rhyme,
Amongst the empty bottles of wine,
There are six people living there,
None of which seems to care!

Kate Moscardini (10)
Newport Community Primary School

TEDDY BEAR

I have got a teddy bear
Who's going very bald,
I take him everywhere
because he's very old.
He is fraying at the seams
But he doesn't really mind;
He keeps me safe in my dreams,
He's also very kind.
His eyes are falling off,
His ears need sewing on,
He's stuffed with lots of fluff
But he's still quite strong.
Every time I see him
Sitting on my bed at night,
I often think, without him
What would life be like?
He's such a special friend
Very dear to my heart
He's been my best friend
From the very start.

Jessica White (10)
Newport Community Primary School

BACK TO SCHOOL

Homework - haven't done it,
PE bag - left it at home,
Reading book - dog chewed it,
Must have thought it was a bone.

Jumper - forgot to wash,
T-shirt - didn't name,
Trousers - lost last term,
Well, this is what I claim!

Pencils - forgot to sharpen,
Pens - leaked out in my bag,
Ruler - snapped in half,
Why can school be such a drag?

Zoe Thayre (10)
Newport Community Primary School

POETRY COMPETITION

There was a poetry competition;
I really wanted mine to win,
I tried hard, but every idea I had
Ended up in the rubbish bin!

I asked my sisters to help me,
'After I've done my French, maths and history.'
My dad's idea was to base it on
Flowers, trees, plants and greenery.

Mum was in the kitchen, baking cakes,
As I asked her to help me make it rhyme,
The flour bag burst all over the floor,
'Later,' she said, 'when I've more time.'

I sat with the dog - she didn't say much -
And I thought I'd have to give it a miss.
I looked at my page as I chewed my pen,
And smiled as I realised I'd come up with this!

Kayleigh Andrews (11)
Newport Community Primary School

WIND

Silent whisperer
   Leaf rustler
      Kite flyer
         Washing drier

           Water rippler
             Wave roller
          Rain pusher
       Sail blower

     Coat flapper
    Hat snatcher
  Tree shaker
Hurricane maker.

Peter Hill (10)
Newport Community Primary School

ME

PlayStation liker,
Good striker,
TV watcher,
Excellent catcher,
Football smacker,
Naughty snacker,
Love eating cracker,
Good worker,
Biscuit tin lurker.

Joe Hunter (9)
Newport Community Primary School

ORIE

There was a girl called Orie,
She was crying on her own,
Her mummy came with a lollipop
And Orie ran straight home.

She was crying for a reason,
A bee had stung her on her arm.
She showed her mummy where it hurt,
And her mummy said 'Stay calm!'

Orie's mummy got some vinegar
And dabbed it on her arm,
She told Orie not to worry
'Cause bees don't do much harm.

She kissed Orie better
And told her to go out to play.
'You don't want to stay in
On this lovely sunny day.'

As Orie was going out to play
She saw another bee!
She ran back inside, crying,
'It's coming after me!'

'Don't be silly!' her mummy said,
'The bee's not after you.'
So off she went, but stayed inside,
And found something else to do.

Shauni Draper (9)
Newport Community Primary School

FOOTBALL CRAZY

Football crazy am I.
I play in the morning,
I play in the afternoon,
I play in the evening.
Football crazy am I.
I dream football when sleeping,
I dream football at school,
I dream football when working,
Football mad am I.
I love Liverpool,
Liverpool are the best team,
I love playing football,
I love watching football on the TV.
I wish I could eat football,
I wish I could drink football,
I wish I was a football player,
I wish I was Michael Owen,
I wish I could go and see Liverpool play,
I wish I could meet the players,
I would like to be a manager for Liverpool,
I would like to play for Liverpool,
I would like to be a striker for Liverpool,
Football mad am I.
If I could play for Liverpool I could eat
Big Macs all the time.
If I could play football all day I would be the best.
If I was in the crowd I would be the loudest cheerer,
Football crazy am I.

Jamie Easterbrook (9)
Newport Community Primary School

MANCHESTER UNITED

Manchester United on the ball
As they do.
They always score.
What a day we did enjoy!
Even my dad felt like a boy.
The ground stays dry
As the day goes by,
Beckham always knows what to do,
He always knows how to get one through,
Giggsy follows it all the way through,
What a brilliant thing to do.
When I grow up, a footballer I will be,
And then they will all come to see me!

Bradley Barbrook (8)
Newport Community Primary School

THE CUP IS MINE

Football is great
Football is cool
You kick the ball
The keeper dives
he cannot reach.
Goal!
But the other team
Tries to score but can't.
Oh no!
In the last minutes we score.
Wicked!
The final score
Two-nil the cup is mine.

Luke Austen (10)
Pilton Bluecoat Junior School

I'D LIKE TO BE . . .

I'd like to be an astronaut
and fly up to the stars,
or maybe visit Saturn
or Jupiter or Mars.

I'd like to be a tree cutter
and use a huge chainsaw,
I'd tie myself with good strong rope
to make sure I didn't fall.

I'd like to be a fireman
and put out lots of fires,
you would see me drive the engine
and hear the screech of tyres.

I'd like to be a scuba diver
and go swimming with the sharks,
I'd see the fish in shallow pools
and in oceans where it's dark.

But which one shall I choose to be?
I think I'll take my time,
I'll stay at school a little while,
after all I'm only nine!

Jamie Prouse (9)
Pilton Bluecoat Junior School

BLACKIE THE HORSE

Galloping in the wind,
Mane and tail blowing,
My friend Blackie the horse
Is happily neighing!

Hayley Johnson (9)
Pilton Bluecoat Junior School

ABOUT BUTTERFLIES

Butterfly, butterfly in the air,
How lovely is that coat you wear.
Flying in the sunny sky,
Your wings flutter as you go by.
Red and blue, purple and green.
Flying past,
But where have you been?

Faye Young (8)
Pilton Bluecoat Junior School

SPIDERS

Spiders, spiders everywhere,
Spiders,
Spiders in your hair,
Spiders in the kitchen,
Spiders in the lounge,
Spiders sure do hang around,
Spiders make their home anywhere,
Because they don't really *care!*

Kealeigh Roddis (9)
Pilton Bluecoat Junior School

POLAR BEAR

Polar bear, polar bear
How do you keep clean?
I seem to get so dirty just walking near a stream

Polar bear, polar bear
How do you bath?
I seem to get so dirty just walking down my path.

So polar bear, polar bear
Help me dear polar bear
I'm dying to know.

Elaine Loveridge (9)
Pilton Bluecoat Junior School

THE GOLDFISH

Neither legs nor arms have I
But I swim across the water
And I blow
   bubbles bubbles bubbles

Neither horns nor hooves have I
But I have a tail
And I blow
   bubbles bubbles bubbles

Neither bows nor guns have I
I dash under the rocks
And I blow
   bubbles bubbles bubbles

Neither radar nor missiles have I
But I stare with my eyes
And I blow
   bubbles bubbles bubbles

I master every moment
For I swim swim swim
And I blow
   bubbles bubbles bubbles.

Sophie Winfield (10)
Pilton Bluecoat Junior School

DOUBLE TROUBLE

You know what happens with twins
They always do the same
But there's always an older one
And the youngest gets the blame.

You know what happens with twins
They do really weird things
They jump up and down together
And do kicks, rolls and spins.

You know what happens with twins
They always do the same
But if they were to swap
Then who would get the blame?

Kathryn Marie Venn Munns (9)
Pilton Bluecoat Junior School

THERE'S A SPIDER ON MY CHAIR

There's a spider on my chair
I wonder how it got there
Did it climb or did it swing?
Please take away that horrible thing
Squash it dead, that's my plot
Now I can show my friends
What I've got.

Sam Furse (8)
Pilton Bluecoat Junior School

THE FIGHT

There is a boy
In my school
He really is a great big fool
He thinks he's flown an aeroplane
He thinks he's done it all
I hate the boy who's up all night
Studying and thinks he's done it right
He really is a great big fool
And so one day we had a fight
He just thought he might win
Because he thinks he knows it all
I punched him on the forehead
He hit me on the nose
I pinned him by the door
He threw me on the floor
I said to myself hold in the tears.
He beat me once
I'll beat him twice, even more
But he still thinks he's done it all
Still he is a great big fool.

Pippa Friend (11)
Pilton Bluecoat Junior School

BOYS

Boys, boys,
They get everywhere.
In your hair,
On your nerves,
Like devils in the air.
Boys, boys
Are everywhere.

Jadine Watson (8)
Pilton Bluecoat Junior School

SANDALS

My sandals are so squidgy
My sandals are so nice
I like to wear them all the time
They are better than eating rice

I wear them when I go to sleep
They're orange, green and red.
I'm never without my sandals
They sometimes even get fed!

Hannah Cluley (9)
Pilton Bluecoat Junior School

A BIRD

I would like to be a bird,
So I could fly,
Over the hills high in the sky.
To spread my wings and glide,
All over the countryside.
To perch upon a tree,
Oh what a wonderful life
It would be.

Jody Fewings (8)
Pilton Bluecoat Junior School

AUTUMN WITCHES

Here comes the witches,
The autumn witches.
They take the leaves off the trees
And make it freezing cold!

Their wands make the leaves crisp,
They turn them into lots of colours,
It turns all frosty.
It gives you frosty breath!

Snapping twigs bite at their ankles
Trying to save the precious leaves.
The witches rustle through the leaves;
They're working on their mission.

Here they come
Back to the cave where they hibernate
Until next autumn
And now the winter bites come.

James Cann (11)
Pilton Bluecoat Junior School

THE LIFE OF A FROG

Frogs are slimy and slippery too
They croak and croak all day long
Jumping on lily pads
Croaking their song.

Frogs are green
With four webbed feet
They have got bumpy backs
And they are nice to meet.

First they are frog spawn
Then comes the tadpoles
Next is the little frogs
Jumping all over my lawn.

Rebecca Cooke (11)
Pilton Bluecoat Junior School

FOOTBALL CRAZE

Football! Football! Football!
All they do is kick a ball.
Most people are tall and small.
When they play they seem to be cool.
Football's boring
And nobody seems to do any scoring.
Ever!

Roxanne Kerner (9)
Pilton Bluecoat Junior School

AUTUMN

All different colours of leaves
blowing in the cool breeze,
crunching, crackling rustling leaves
Falling from the trees

Swirling, whirling
Spinning round
Slowly falling to the ground

Brown, yellow, red, green
These are all colours
From an autumn theme.

Mikayla Brookes (11)
Pilton Bluecoat Junior School

TEN CROSS TEACHERS

Ten cross teachers all drinking wine
One drank too much then there were nine

Nine cross teachers one was late
She fell over then there were eight
Eight cross teachers two had too much Weetabix
Then went crazy then there were six

Six cross teachers all alive
But one died of shock then there were five

Five cross teachers all saw a bee
Two got stung then there were three

Three cross teachers all going boo!
One got too grumpy then there were two

Two cross teachers one sang a song
Smashed the windows then there was one

One cross teacher ate a bun
It was poisoned then there were none.

Louise Mason (9)
Pilton Bluecoat Junior School

SPOOKS

Spooks, spooks everywhere.
In your cupboard
And in your hair.

They tickle your head
And scare you in bed.

Then they give you a fright,
In the middle of the night,
But at least they don't bite.

Sweet dreams. Goodnight.

Kirsty Burge (7)
Pilton Bluecoat Junior School

STARS

Gold stars, old stars,
Silver stars, new stars.
Green stars, purple stars.
No such thing.
Shooting stars floating off to the moon.
I heard a rocket is
Taking off soon.

Hannah Bowden (8)
Pilton Bluecoat Junior School

THE ALIENS I KNOW

The aliens I know are a funny lot,
They don't understand all the things they've got,
Like invisible rays and X-ray sight,
And being able to read people's minds.
Now if I could have all those things,
I would be the cleverest girl you could find.
I could read the answers in the teacher's book,
Find all the best things with just one look.
But the best of all I would know,
Where my mum wants me to go.
And be back before she could say
We've got to go to the shops today.

Leanne Dean (9)
Pilton Bluecoat Junior School

MUM, DAD AND ME

My mum is an alien
She really does strange things.
She dances with the vacuum cleaner
When she spring cleans.

My dad he is a nutcase,
As mad as anyone could be.
he's always shouting out my name
And embarrassing me.

Considering my parents
I think I'm quite normal,
Whatever normal is.
I think I'll go upstairs now
To brush my fairy wings.

Katherine Marshall (10)
Pilton Bluecoat Junior School

COOL CAMPSITE

Today I'm staying at a campsite we are putting up a tent
I have to get out all the poles and make sure they're not bent
When the tent's up we need to light candles so the place looks bright
At night I'm scared, people walk past and it gives me a fright

I have to sleep in a sleeping bag 'cause it's very, very cold
My teddy also shares a sleeping bag with me and he is very old.
Sometimes I meet up together with friends and mates
We all go to activity clubs to do art and then go to fetes.

After that we go to a cafe and buy some lovely lunch
Then I go to feed an apple to a pony so he can munch
Then there's a puppet show that is very very funny
After that I get an ice cream soda that's melting and getting all runny
I am so hot and sweaty because it is so sunny

I get into my costume and feel very cool
So I take a big leap and dive in the pool
After a long day I'm very tired so I go to bed and have a little nap
The next day I enter a treasure hunt with the help of a map!

Kelly Watts (9)
Pilton Bluecoat Junior School

LESSONS AT SCHOOL!

Maths is cool,
You do it in school!
English is boring,
You don't do drawing!
Music is smart,
You play your part!
Just accept it,
School is cool,
And if you can't accept that,
Then play by the rules!

Imogen Curtis (9)
Pilton Bluecoat Junior School

I Wish I Were A Cat

I wish I were a cat,
Sleeping all day,
Waking up when I want,
Just to eat and play,
Affection when I need it,
Alone if I want to be,
That would be the life for me.

Gina Corti (10)
Pilton Bluecoat Junior School

WINTER SNOW

Speaking high speaking low,
moving swiftly through the snow.

Slipping here slipping there,
feeling like a polar bear.

Jumping high jumping low,
making footprints in the snow.

Freezing here freezing there,
having fun in the bitter cold air.

Stacey Vaughan (11)
Pilton Bluecoat Junior School

THE MOON TRAVELLER

I travelled to the end of the Earth by sea,
Oh, what a wonderful trip this will be!
Suddenly I lift up really high,
Sailing up across the sky.
I sail past the stars, the moon and the sun,
Well, golly gosh, this is quite fun!
I sail to a planet known as Mars,
And talk to the alien who studies the stars.
I sail up to the man in the moon,
And promise him I'll come back soon.
I sail back home in the pouring rain,
I'll definitely go back there again!

Susannah R E Bay (9)
Pilton Bluecoat Junior School

POEM HOMEWORK

This homework's so annoying I just can't get it done
There ain't no time for it, it's just no fun
This homework's so annoying I'm in despair
This homework's so annoying I'm ripping out my hair
I need to find a poem but where could it be?
I've looked through lots of libraries from A to Z
I guess I won't find a poem but just a minute wait
I've just written one right now so isn't that great!

Mark Wonnacott (10)
Sticklepath Primary School

WILDLIFE

Lions in the jungle
Tigers in a bundle
Ostrich in the mere
Leopard coming near
Whale in the ocean
Swimming in slow motion
Can you see a camel
And there's a mammal
Cute little bear
Breathing in fresh air
Hyenas are laughing
Turtles are bathing
Pandas eating bamboo
Gorilla beating people
Chimp with a knife

I'm talking about *wildlife!*

Jessica Billson (11)
Sticklepath Primary School

IN MY BOX

In my box I will put
A flamingo to watch the tide go by
A crocodile to guard the sun
And a snake to wriggle by

On my box I will put
Hinges made from silver
The skin of a snake
And the eye of a kitten.

Rebecca Louise Derbyshire (11)
Sticklepath Primary School

Dr Dre

Dr Dre is a rapper and that's no word of a lie!
Dr Dre is famous and that's no word of a lie!
Dr Dre is a gangster and that's no word of a lie!
Dr Dre is rude and that's no word of a lie!
Dr Dre sings Next Episode and that's no word of a lie!
Dr Dre sings with Eminem and that's no word of a lie!
Dr Dre lives in the USA and that's no word of a lie!
Dr Dre is the greatest and that's no word of a lie!

Gavin Andrew (10)
Sticklepath Primary School

THE SPORT

The peace and quiet
The only noise
I hear a whistle blown
Get ready set
Bang!
I'm off
I am in the lead
I'm getting closer
The finish line comes closer and closer
My heart beating as I go over the line
And I came first.

Veronica Holland (11)
Sticklepath Primary School

THE CHIMPS

Two little chimps sitting in a tree
One named Bam and one named Bee

They both love to sit in a tree
Watching the birdies go *che che*

Two little chimps sitting in a tree
One named Bam and one named Bee

Eating fruit as cute as can be
They're not stupid, they're just happy!

Two little chimps sitting in a tree
One named Bam and one named Bee

Two little chimps they do what I say
No matter what, they won't run away!

Zoe Simmonds (11)
Sticklepath Primary School

MY CAT KIZZY

My cat Kizzy she's a Kung Fu kitty,
She eats a tonne of meat and always acts so sweet.

My cat Kizzy she's a Kung Fu kitty,
She runs around all day
And never runs away.

My cat Kizzy she's a Kung Fu kitty,
She eats a tonne of meat and always acts so sweet.

My cat Kizzy she's a Kung Fu kitty,
She sleeps in at night and then she catches a bite.

My cat Kizzy she's a Kung Fu kitty,
She eats a tonne of meat and always acts so sweet.

My cat Kizzy she's a Kung Fu kitty,
She has smoky coloured fur
And always does her little purr.

Lucy Sleeman (10)
Sticklepath Primary School

STRETCH YOUR IMAGINATION

Stretch your imagination
Go beyond walls.
Stretch your imagination
Go to the Niagara Falls.
Stretch your imagination
Go to the park.
Stretch your imagination
Don't end up in the dark.
Stretch your imagination
Go to space.
Stretch your imagination
Beat Linford Christie's pace.

Simon Hanson (10)
Sticklepath Primary School

ALL ABOUT MY MUM

My mum is very healthy
My mum is very cool
My mum has a bath every afternoon
She goes out every Wednesday
She has spiked hair
Whenever she puts make-up on
She gives everybody a scare
She comes down in the mornings
Like an elephant on his knee
Then she goes to town on Saturday
And drinks lots of tea.

Natalie Elston (10)
Sticklepath Primary School

MY DAD

My dad is very old,
He is very very bald,
When he's out in the car
He always travels very far.

On the way to his work
He always hears a dog bark.
At five o'clock he comes home
And he has a bath and sings
Like a monkey.

Five minutes later he gets out
And he walks about.
Two days later he becomes ill
And he always takes a pill.

Robert Lewis (10)
Sticklepath Primary School

THE DIRTY BULLDOG

The dirty bulldog likes to rummage in mud
But when he gets dirty he gets really mad.
He starts getting fierce but cats scare him off.
He gets really lonely and starts to cry.
But then jumps in the mud and starts to play
He decides he's only got one friend and that is
the mud!

Sam McCreadie (11)
Sticklepath Primary School

DOCTOR

My doctor's funny, my doctor's weird
My doctor's got a long funny beard

I sat in a chair he looks at me
And said I have a dislocated knee
'What shall I do about my knee'
I asked politely
'We could wrap it up, strap it up, push it in punch it in
What do you want me to do?'

My doctor's funny, my doctor's weird
My doctor's got a long funny beard

'I think it is fine Doctor, I think it is scarred'
No it is not dear this is very hard
I came out of hospital with crutches and a sticker
Got in the car and everyone started to bicker.

My doctor's funny, my doctor's weird
My doctor's got a long funny beard.

Lydia Brown (11)
Sticklepath Primary School

THE LITTLE RABBIT

The little white rabbit bouncing around,
Trying not to make a sound.
Then he sees a tasty carrot,
Making sure there's not a parrot,
He takes the carrot
And brings it to his friends.
The little rabbit small as a mouse,
Looking for his house.
When he finds his little house
Then he will have dinner with the louse.

Natalie Dundh (10)
Two Moors Primary School

SPRINGTIME

I see the sun beaming down on me,
The creatures are having their morning stroll.
The dead bones of a flower surrounds me,
The trees are waking up ready for spring.

Flowers are blooming to be seen,
Sweet smells of fruit coming from the trees.
Bulbs are growing to make new plants,
The grass is wet and soggy.

Trees are growing new leaves,
The misty fields are clearing up.
The ice in the pond is melting,
Animals are coming out of their burrows.

The tired bushes are slowly waking up,
Dead bushes start to grow back.
Frozen leaves slowly melting,
The spring is here.

Tom Hawkins (11)
Two Moors Primary School

GROWING UP IN NUMBERS

Ten bouncing babies
Looking extremely fine,
One needed a nappy change
Then there were nine.

Nine tiny toddlers
At the school fete,
One got lost
Then there were eight.

Eight crazy kids
Sunbathing in Devon,
One got sunburnt
Then there were seven.

Seven joyful juniors
All having a Twix,
One had Weetabix
And then there were six.

Six troublesome teenagers
All taking dives,
One did a belly-flop
And then there were five.

Five anxious adults
Breaking the law,
One got arrested
Then there were four.

Four grumpy grandpas
Dancing round a tree,
One needed a wee
Then there were three.

Three great grandpas
Eating vindaloo,
One needed the loo
Then there were two.

Two scary skeletons
Drinking lots of rum
One got drunk
Then there was one.

One spooky spirit
Trying to be a hero
Accidentally punched
Himself then there
Were zero.

Class E2 (7/8)
Two Moors Primary School

DR NICE

I went to the Dr, Dr Nice to pay a visit . . .
because I had lice.
Then Dr Nice gave me a hit,
because I was a silly old twit!

Sophie Andrews (11)
Two Moors Primary School

PIRATES

Our ship goes along
On the rough, choppy seas,
The crew are all lazy
(They love mushy peas!)

But out of the blue
Comes up a pirate ship
'Oh Lord!' cries a sailor
'I think I will flip!'

'I'm too young to die!'
Yells another young skip,
'Please help me get away
From this pirate ship!'

The ship came up closer
The crew ran away
They sailed to an island
Right up to the bay.

They then all got up
And got off the boat,
'I don't like this island
It's awfully remote!'

'I s'ppose it will do
Just for a while.'
Said yet another sailor
Who was growing a smile.

The pirates went away
And never came back,
The sailors built a cabin
They called it 'The Shack'.

Thomas Drysdale (11)
Two Moors Primary School

MY TWIN BROTHER

My twin brother is so annoying,
In the morning he jumps on my bed,
And yells in my ear
'Wake up you sleepy head!'

Then in breakfast he yells again,
'We're late for school . . .
Come on you fool.'
That's why my brother is so annoying.

Sammy Head (11)
Two Moors Primary School

UNTITLED

In the house there is a mouse
She's looking very hairy.
Up the stair and everywhere
Her name is baby Mary.

Lyndsay Rachel Ryan (11)
Two Moors Primary School

THE BRINGER OF DEATH

The death toll is high
The man who did this, said 'Why?'
They were thieving scum

My name is Hitler
I live to kill, that means you
I hate Gypsies

Jews are just as bad
The gas chambers are the best
They die very slowly

They all must die slow
I almost conquered Europe
I am a dead man.

Thomas Hutter (11)
Two Moors Primary School

SPRING WALK

Cold and icy morning,
Blackbirds whistling,
Misty grass all around,
Squishy, squelchy soggy brown mud.

Frosty branches sitting in the playground,
Tadpoles spreading around the pond,
Yellow, red and brown sparkling branches,
Buds appearing on the wet branches.

Ashes dying down grey black and brown,
Leaves dying down and spreading on the ground,
Basketball nets blowing in the wind,
Wet mouldy and slippery logs.

Powerful sun shining on us.

Vicky Preston (11)
Two Moors Primary School

SPRING

The face wakes to a cold morning,
Happily melting the ice,
As the wind blows smoke rings.

Trees yawn like children,
Buds sprout,
Whilst black dots scurry over them.

Spiky hair pops from the soil,
Trying to find the sunlight,
So they bloom.

Spring is here,
I can't wait
Till next year.

Ben Daniel (10)
Two Moors Primary School

WHITE SKY

She spreads as far as the eye can see
Following a trail left by he
She dances away so very fast
Her visit never seems to last

Her sparkling eyes glint and gleam
Nothing is ever what it seems
She twirls and swirls high above
The colour of a bright white dove

The midnight air is cool and crisp
From far beyond a ghostly wisp
A whitened plume forever flies
The snowflake's spirit never dies.

Jordan Thomas (10)
Two Moors Primary School

My Brother

My brother really annoys me,
But what can I do,
He's older and in high school,
He's bigger than me too.

My brother really enjoys
What he's doing to me,
But one day I'll get my own back,
Just you wait and see.

Zoe Bates (10)
Two Moors Primary School

MUM'S BIRTHDAY

It is my mum's birthday
Some time in July,
I don't know what to get her,
Perhaps an apple pie.

I asked my dad what she liked,
He said 'Don't ask me,'
I know what I'll get her,
A big bag of tea.

I thought about a kitten,
I thought about a flea,
I thought about an elephant,
But not from me.

It's hopeless now, I just can't think,
I'll just have to paint the bathroom sink,
So I'll go outside now and cut a log,
I know what I'll get her, a spotty dog!

Alice Bennett (10)
Two Moors Primary School

SPRINGTIME

Cold winds
Smoky breath
Frozen grass.

Bulbs growing to make new plants.
Creatures having morning strolls,
The sun is rising over the hills.

The branches wet and soggy,
Wet slimy trunks,
Muddy hard leaves.

Blue sky,
Misty air,
Sparkling grass.

Trevor Davis (11)
Two Moors Primary School

MY FAMILY

My mum is dumb,
My dad is mad,
I am just a kind little lad.

My sister is forgetful,
My brother is a geek,
I am always cheerful, every day of the week.

My grandad is always talking about the war,
Really, he is just a bore,
When he's talking I begin to snore.

My auntie is always chat chat chat,
My uncle is fat,
They think I'm a rat.

But I'm not,
I am just a regular boy,
And I am pleased with what I've got.

My family is a weird one,
And sometimes rather mad,
But if I did not know them,
I would be rather sad.

Andrew Jones (11)
Two Moors Primary School